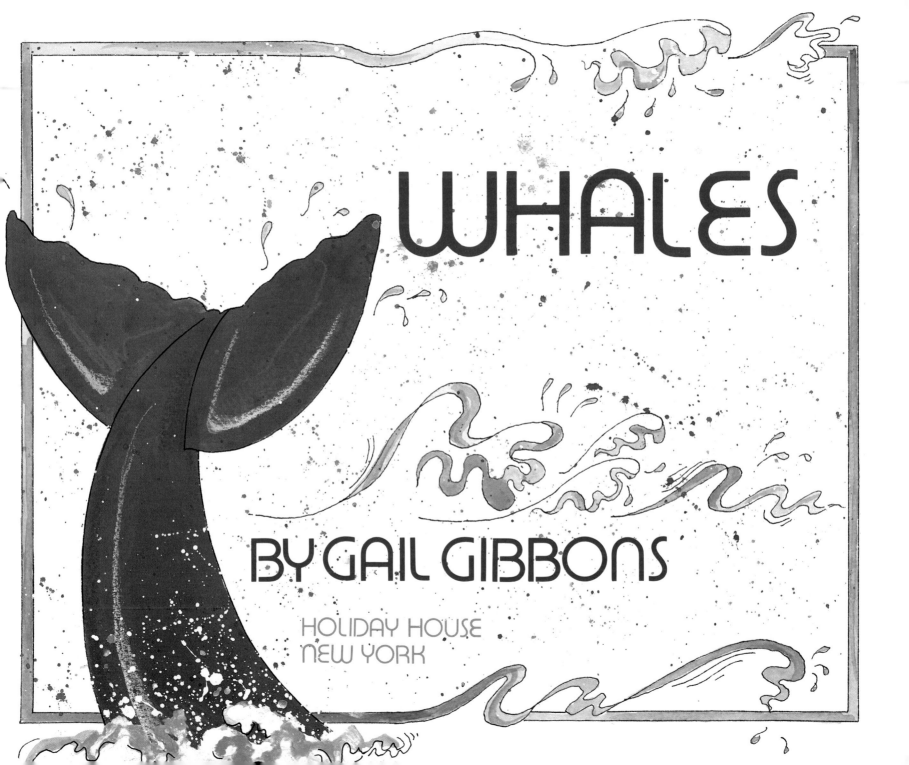

WHALES

BY GAIL GIBBONS

HOLIDAY HOUSE
NEW YORK

For Karen, Peter and
Kirsten Collins

Special thanks to Dr. Richard H. Tedford of the
American Museum of Natural History, New York

Copyright © 1991 by Gail Gibbons
Printed in the United States of America

Library of Congress Cataloging-in-Publication Data
Gibbons, Gail.
Whales / by Gail Gibbons.
p.   cm.
Summary: Introduces different kinds of whales.
ISBN 0-8234-0900-7
1. Whales—Juvenile literature.   [1. Whales.]   I. Title.
QL737.C4G37   1991   91-4507   CIP   AC
599.5—dc20
ISBN 0-8234-1030-7 (pbk.)

Whales live in oceans. They are not fish. They are
air-breathing, warmblooded mammals.

Some are small, and others are huge!

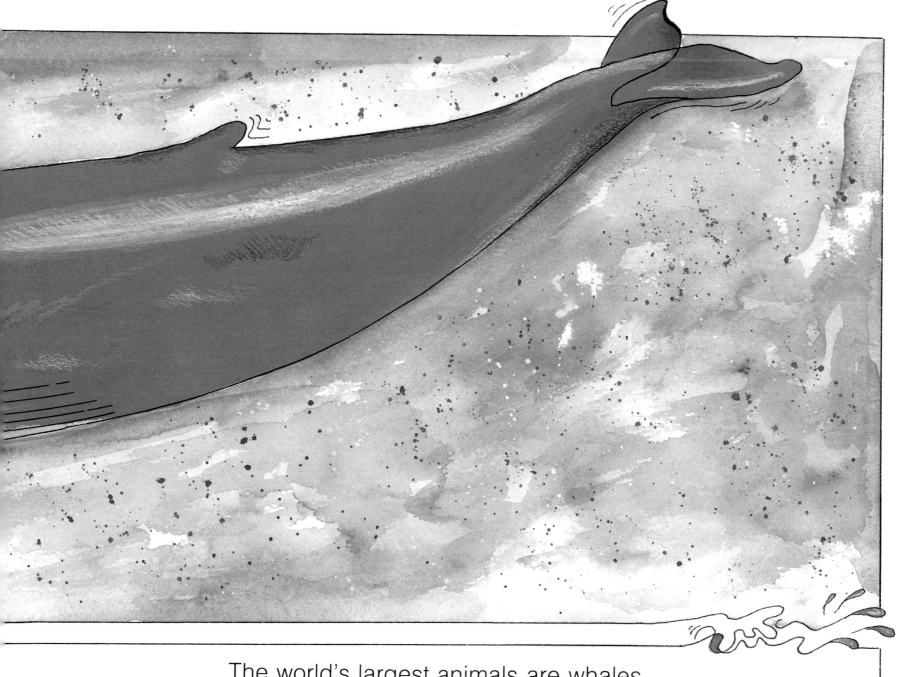

The world's largest animals are whales.

MESONYCHID
mes o NICK id

The first ancestors of whales lived more than 50 million years ago. Scientists believe they are descended from creatures that lived on land, possibly the mesonychid.

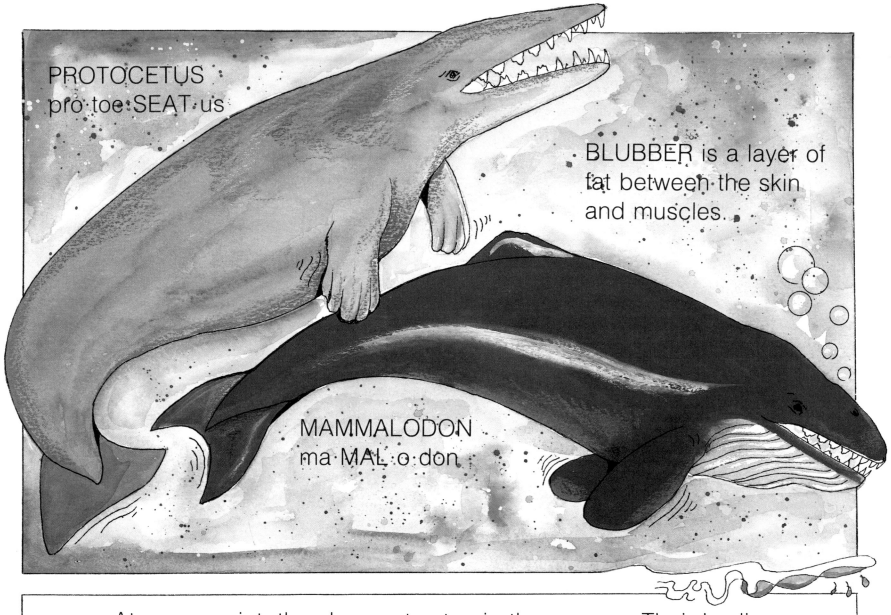

PROTOCETUS
pro·toe·SEAT·us

BLUBBER is a layer of
fat between the skin
and muscles.

MAMMALODON
ma·MAL·o·don

At some point, they began to stay in the oceans. Their bodies
became more streamlined for easier swimming. Their fur was
replaced by blubber to keep them warm.

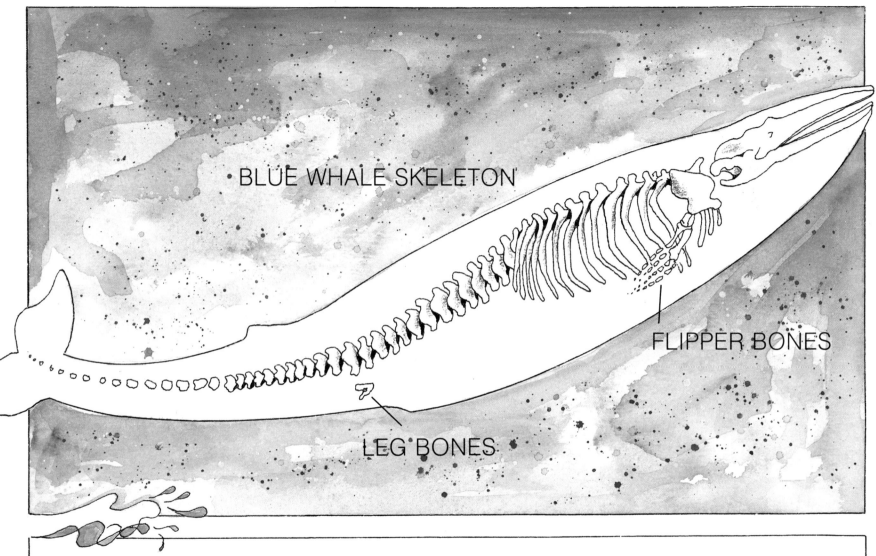

BLUE WHALE SKELETON

FLIPPER BONES

LEG BONES

Today, millions of years later, skeletons of whales show clues to their early ancestors. Inside their flippers are bones arranged like those of a hand. Further back there are remains of small leg bones, but there are no flippers here.

FLUKE

FLIPPER

Whales' tails are called flukes. They don't look like fish tails. Whales push themselves through the water by moving their flukes up and down. They use their flippers for balance and turning.

BLOWHOLE

Whales can't stay under water like fish. Beneath the surface they must hold their breath. Before diving, whales breathe fresh air into their lungs through one or two nostrils on top of their heads. They are called blowholes.

—SPOUT

When whales surface, they blow out their wet, warm breath, making a spout.

SONAR or
ECHOLOCATION
ek·o·low·KAY·shun

When whales can't see well in dark and murky waters, they make clicking sounds. The sound waves travel and bounce off objects. Then they come back to the whales' ears. This is called sonar or echolocation.

Some whales make other sounds, too. They resemble squeals, groans, chirps and whistles like birds. Scientists believe that whales make these sounds to communicate with each other.

MIGRATION
my·GRAY·shun

POD

Some whales travel to cold waters to feed and live in the summer. Often they travel in groups, called pods. In the winter they go back to the warmer waters. This traveling is called migration.

COW

BULL

A CALF NURSING

In the warm waters, the females have their babies. They can only have one baby at a time. A male is called a bull and a female is called a cow. A baby is called a calf.

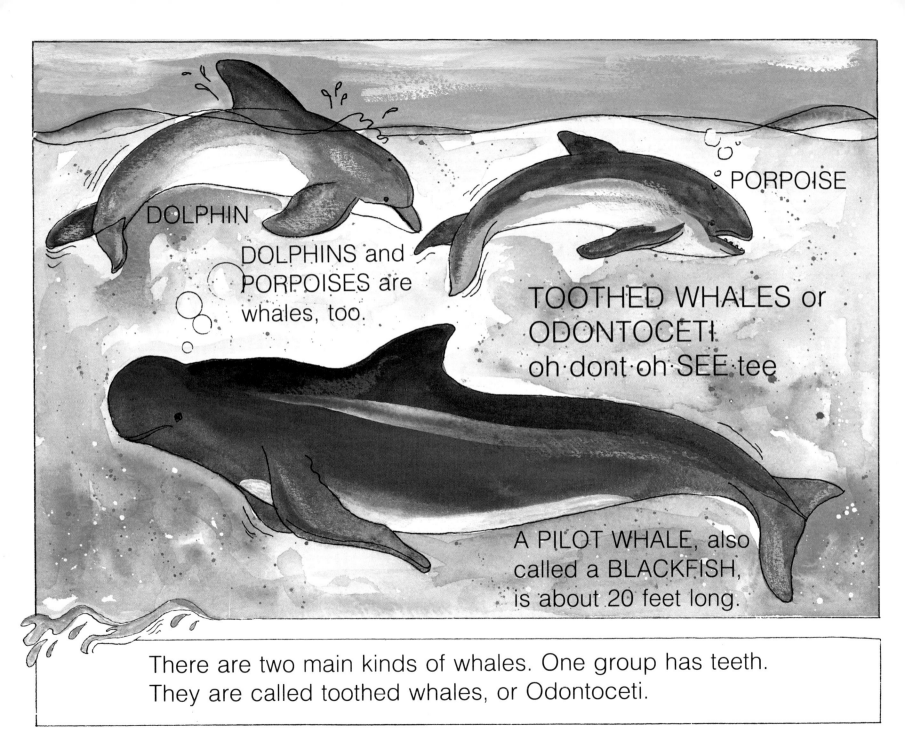

DOLPHIN

PORPOISE

DOLPHINS and PORPOISES are whales, too.

TOOTHED WHALES or ODONTOCETI
oh dont oh SEE tee

A PILOT WHALE, also called a BLACKFISH, is about 20 feet long.

There are two main kinds of whales. One group has teeth.
They are called toothed whales, or Odontoceti.

The NARWHAL has two teeth. In the males, one of the teeth grows into a long tusk.

A BELUGA (bah·LOO·ga), also called a WHITE WHALE, lives near the North Pole. It is about 18 feet long.

Most toothed whale males are larger than the females.

A SPERM WHALE can
stay under water
for a very long time.
It can be 65 feet long.

Toothed whales have only one blowhole.

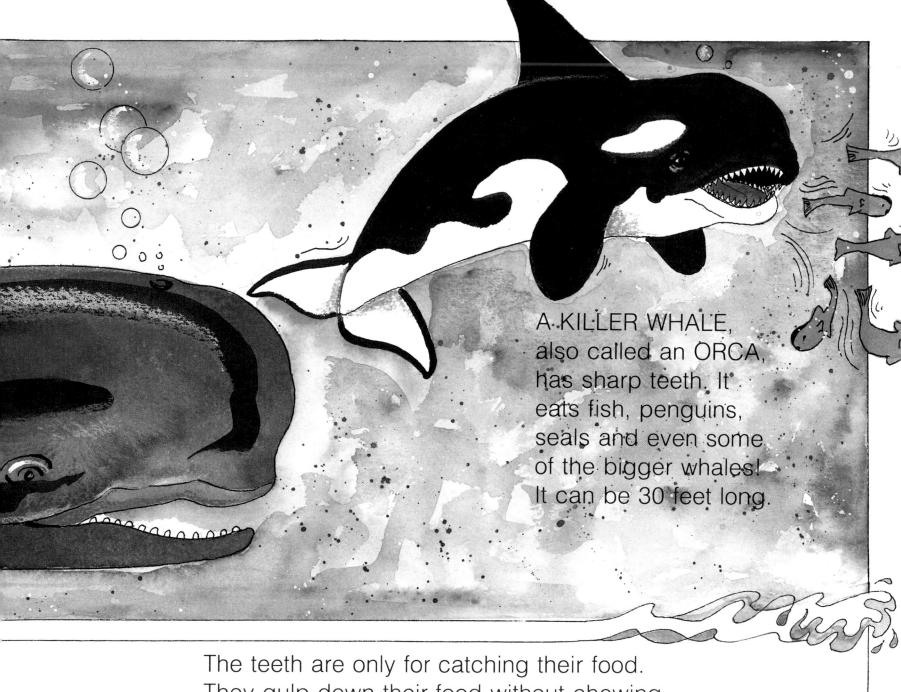

A KILLER WHALE,
also called an ORCA,
has sharp teeth. It
eats fish, penguins,
seals and even some
of the bigger whales!
It can be 30 feet long.

The teeth are only for catching their food.
They gulp down their food without chewing.

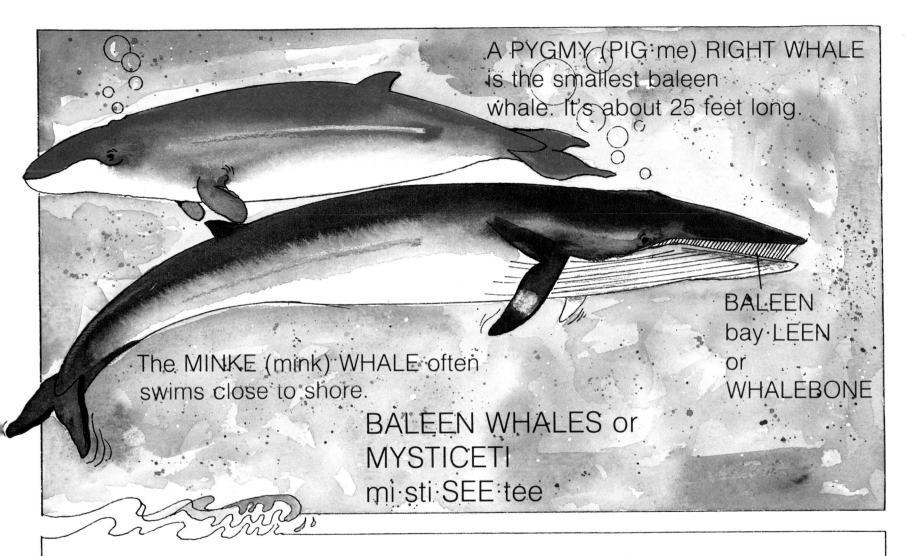

A PYGMY (PIG me) RIGHT WHALE is the smallest baleen whale. It's about 25 feet long.

The MINKE (mink) WHALE often swims close to shore.

BALEEN
bay·LEEN
or
WHALEBONE

BALEEN WHALES or
MYSTICETI
mi·sti·SEE·tee

The other main group of whales has no teeth. Instead, they have long, fringed blades hanging from their upper jaws that strain out their food from the water. The blades are called baleen, or whalebone. Baleen whales are also called Mysticeti.

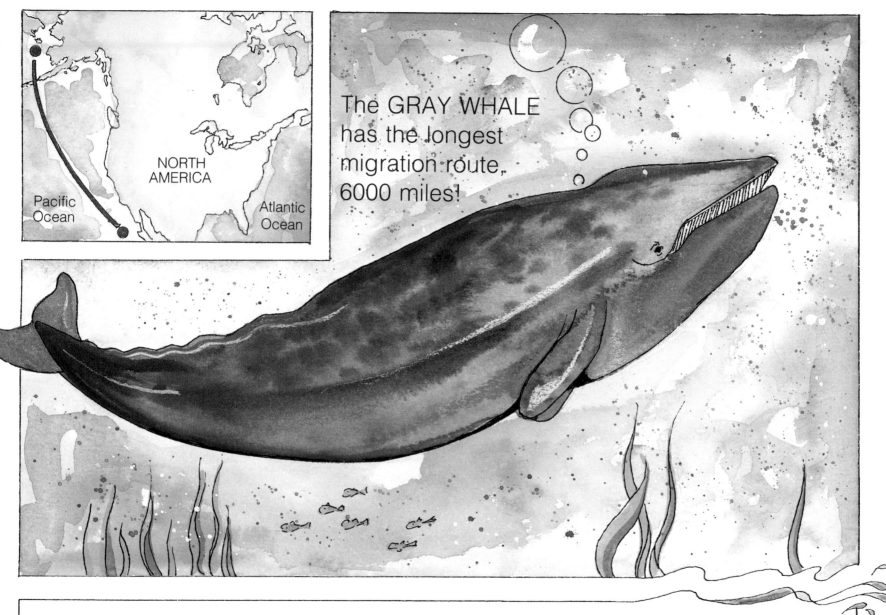

NORTH AMERICA

Pacific Ocean

Atlantic Ocean

The GRAY WHALE has the longest migration route, 6000 miles!

Baleen whales eat fish and a mixture of tiny plants called plankton. In the plankton are shrimplike creatures called krill.

The SEI (say) WHALE is about 60 feet long.

The HUMPBACK WHALE is known for its songs. It can make about 1000 different sounds.

All baleen whales have two blowholes.

A RIGHT WHALE has a huge head and is about 55 feet long.

The female baleen whales are often larger than the males.

The BOWHEAD WHALE,
also called the
GREENLAND RIGHT WHALE,
has the longest baleen
of any whale, 15 feet long.

Baleen whales are among the biggest of the whales.

The FIN WHALE
is huge. It got
its name from the
hooked fin on its
back.

Some baleen whales have grooves on their skin
from their chins to their bellies.

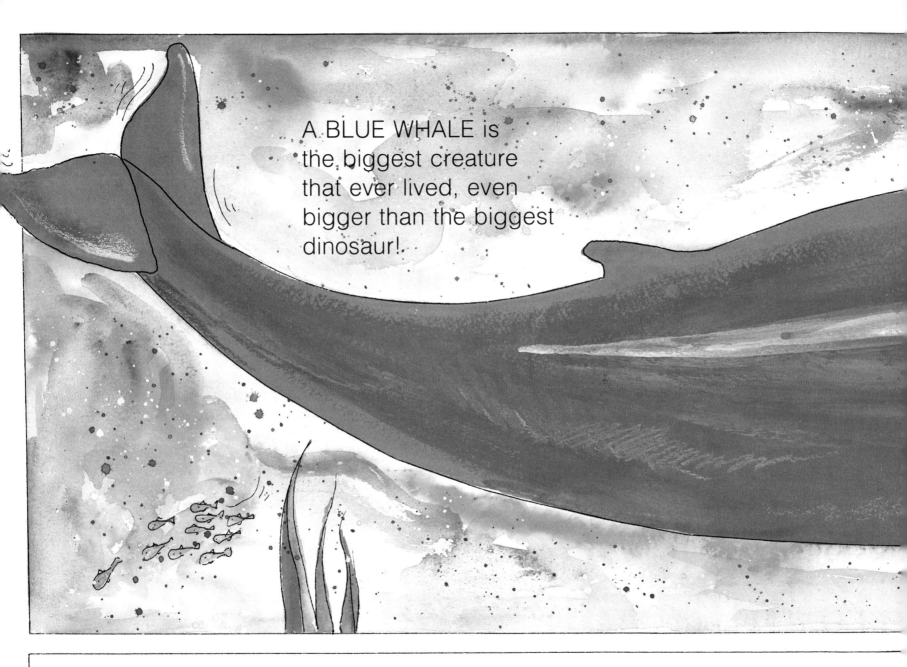

A BLUE WHALE is
the biggest creature
that ever lived, even
bigger than the biggest
dinosaur!

Baleen whales are graceful . . .

It is often
100 feet long and
can weigh as much
as 180 tons.

and peaceful creatures.

There used to be millions of whales in the oceans. For thousands of years they were hunted for their meat, hide and bones. About 200 years ago, whalers began hunting them even more for other products.

They used different parts of whales to make lamp oil, soap, candles and cosmetics. The whalers used the baleen to make buggy whips, umbrellas and stiffening for clothes. Over the years, there were fewer and fewer whales.

Today, people are worried about how small the whale population has become. Some laws have been passed to protect them from being hunted.
Sometimes people go on whale watches to see these creatures in their natural home, the ocean.

Scientists have learned that there are about 100 different kinds of whales. They are graceful and beautiful wonders of the sea.

WHALE TALES

In 1851, Herman Melville wrote a book called *Moby Dick.* It told about a magnificent white sperm whale that whalers were hunting.

A blue whale eats about 4,400 pounds of krill a day.

Now and then whales accidentally swim onto a beach and become stranded. Sometimes, people help them return to the sea so they won't die.

A sperm whale can dive down more than a half mile.

A baby blue whale is the biggest baby in the world. At birth it is about 25 feet long and can weigh 4000 pounds.

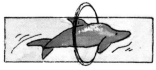

Some whales can be trained to do tricks.

Breaching is when a whale leaps from the water.

A blue whale is so big that 50 people could stand on its tongue.

In 1985, Humphrey the humpback whale became lost and wandered up California's Sacramento River. Scientists lured Humphrey back to sea by playing a tape of humpback whale songs.

In 1990, Humphrey was stranded in San Francisco Bay. Thousands of Humphrey fans watched scientists help him get back out to sea again.

Recorded sounds of humpback whales have been sent into outer space on *Voyager 1* and *2.*